SMALL
MATTERS

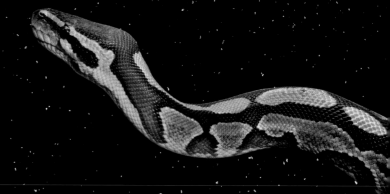

**FOR ANNETTE, AUDRA, AND ERIC,
WHO INSPIRE ME IN WAYS BOTH BIG AND SMALL**

Acknowledgments

Thanks and appreciation to all those who gave me encouragement along the way—
ever-ready writing partners Gabi, Mary, Wendy, Lynne-Ann, Peggy, Kelly, Lisa, and Claire;
scientific consultants Angela Hwang, PhD, Sue Okerstrom (president Lichen Labs LLC), and Emily
Smith; resident rocket scientist Eric Kinser; eagle-eyed editors Carol Hinz and Allison Juda; and
the fine photo research team at Lerner Publishing Group.

Millbrook Press™
An imprint of Lerner Publishing Group, Inc.
241 First Avenue North
Minneapolis, MN 55401 USA

For reading levels and more information, look up this title at www.lernerbooks.com.

Main body text set in King George Light Clean.
Typeface provided by Chank.

Library of Congress Cataloging-in-Publication Data

Names: Kinser, Heather Ferranti, 1967– author.
Title: Small matters : the hidden power of the unseen / Heather Ferranti Kinser.
Description: Minneapolis : Millbrook Press, [2020] | Audience: Age 4–9. | Audience: K to Grade 3. |
    Includes bibliographical references and index.
Identifiers: LCCN 2019013220 (print) | LCCN 2019014306 (ebook) | ISBN 9781541583818 (eb pdf) |
    ISBN 9781541578142 (lb : alk. paper)
Subjects: LCSH: Tissues—Juvenile literature. | Histology—Juvenile literature. | Animals—Juvenile
    literature.
Classification: LCC QL807 (ebook) | LCC QL807 .S55 2020 (print) | DDC 611/.018—dc23

LC record available at https://lccn.loc.gov/2019013220

Manufactured in the United States of America
1-46891-47795-9/10/2019

SMALL MATTERS

THE HIDDEN POWER OF THE UNSEEN

by Heather Ferranti Kinser

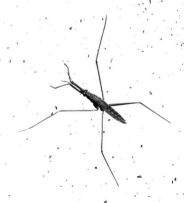

M Millbrook Press/Minneapolis

In a **BIG** world filled with many **BIG** questions, we look for **BIG** answers.

But what if an answer is smaller than small?
Unseen?
Nearly invisible?

Could something *that small* even matter at all?

Let's take a look
with a powerful microscope
that lets us zoom in
on tiny details.

Small things are **STRONG.**

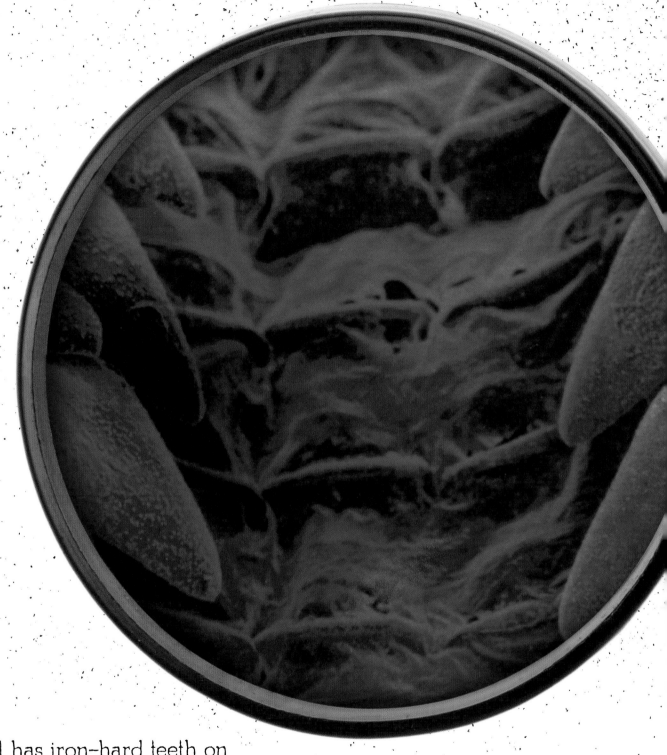

This sea snail has iron-hard teeth on its tongue. The teeth are so strong they can scrape away rock.

Small things
are **SPEEDY.**

A shark's skin is covered in jagged scales that look like tiny teeth with ridges. The scales help this predator slice through the water.

Small things can
CHANGE THE COLORS WE SEE.

Inside a blue morpho butterfly wing, tree-shaped structures bend light, creating colors. Most colors stay trapped. But blue bounces back out in a dazzling shimmer.

Small things can ZIP,

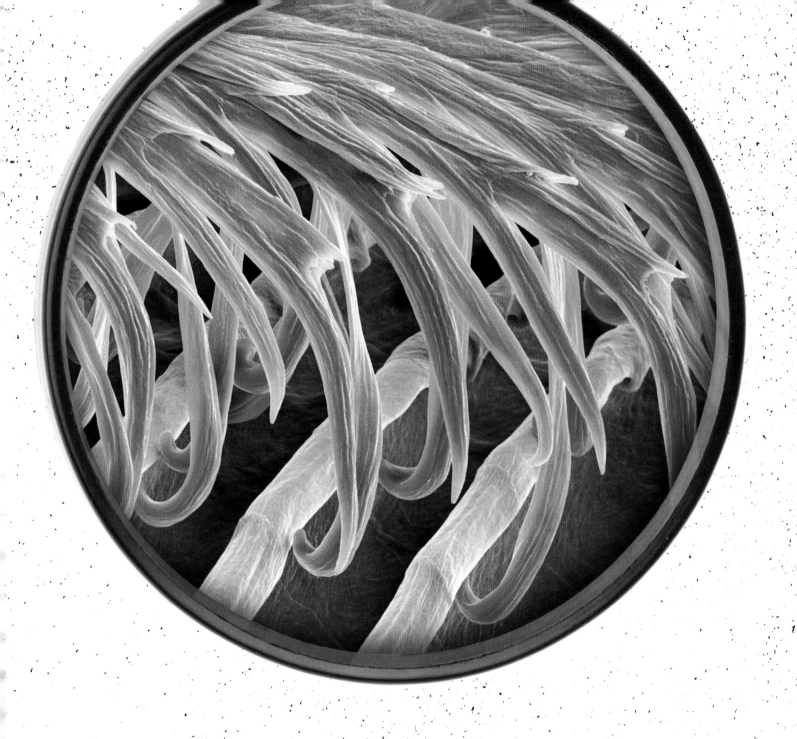

The delicate strands of bird feathers have hooks and grooves that zip together. This keeps the feathers streamlined and sleek, which helps birds fly.

and they can **GRIP.**

Snake bellies are covered in small, toothy ripples that grip at the ground like the treads of a shoe. These ragged edges help the snake slither without slipping backward.

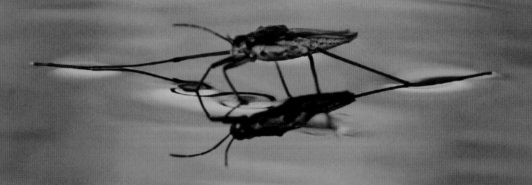

Small things can **HOLD UP** things that are bigger

A water strider walks on water. Its long legs are covered in supersmall hairs that press on the surface without breaking through.

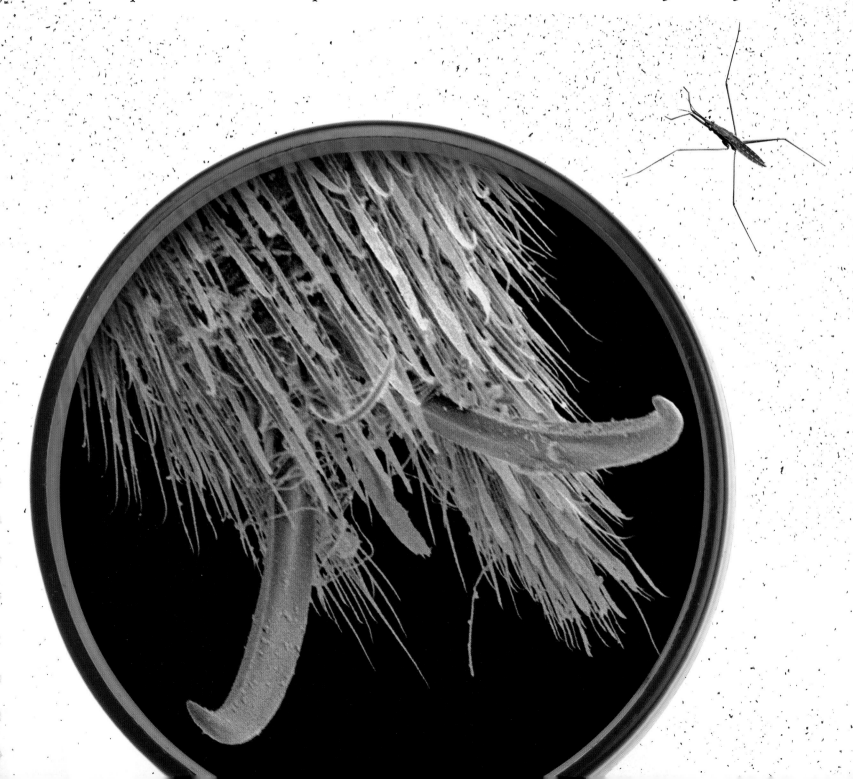

or **HOLD OFF** things that might cause trouble.

A honeybee is fuzzy everywhere. Hairs on its eyes block pollen grains from sticking to the bee's eyes as it bumbles in flowers.

Small things help animals
TIDY UP and **PREEN,**

A cat's tongue is covered in curvy spines. The spines work like a natural comb to untangle knots and gather loose fur.

and stay **DRY** and **CLEAN.**

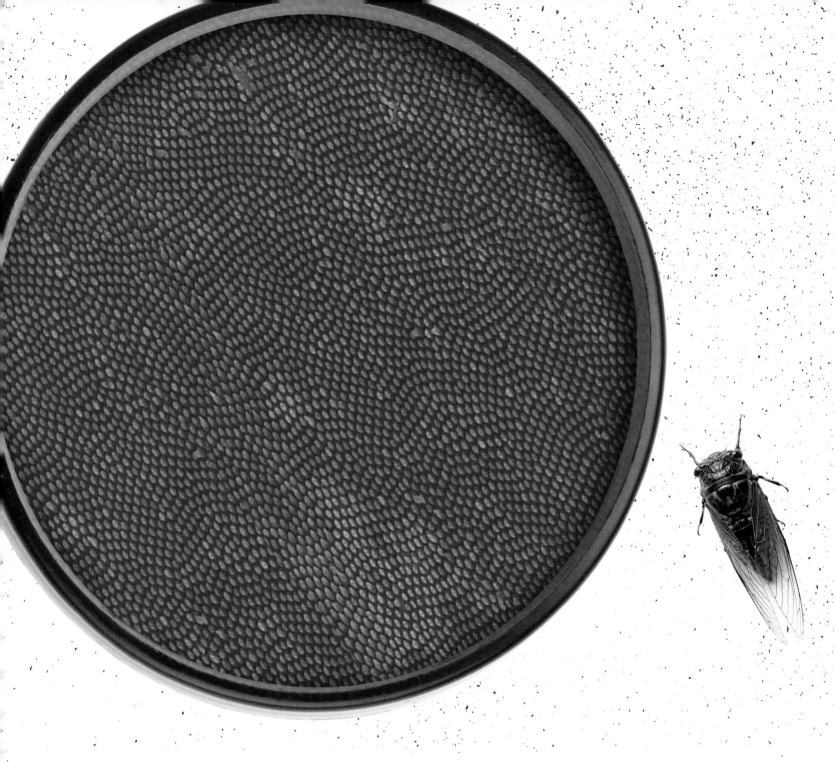

Supersmall bumps on cicada wings cause water to bead up on the wings' surface. When the droplets grow larger, off they pop, leaving the wings neatly washed.

Small things **SUPPORT**, so large things can be light.

A toucan's huge beak is filled with holes like a block of foam. The holes are covered by ultrathin films, which make the beak strong without weighing the bird down.

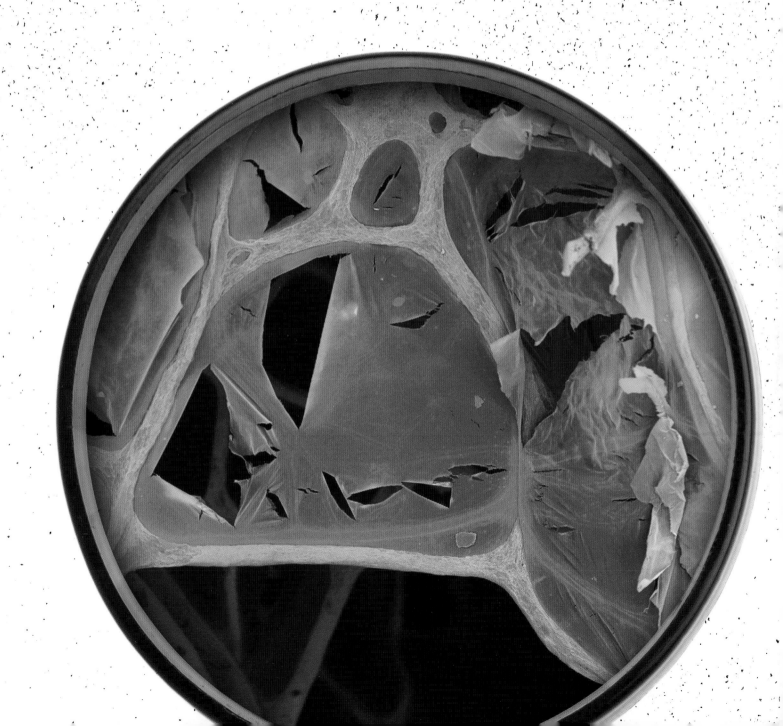

Small things can harness incredible **FORCES!**

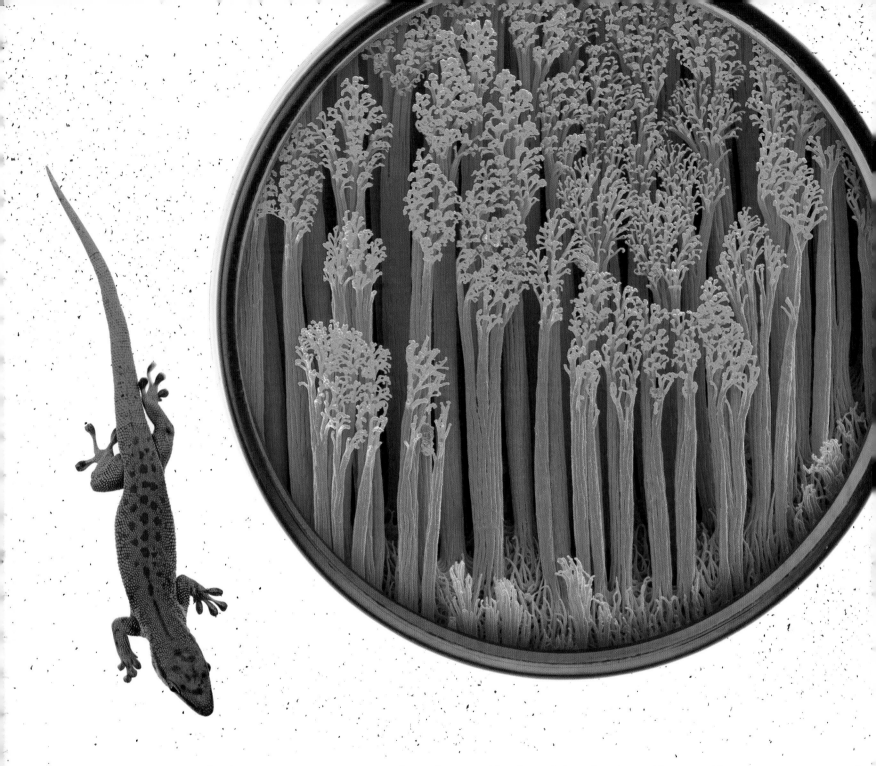

A gecko's toes are covered in hairs that split into bristles with pads at their tips. These pads get incredibly close to a surface and cling with the help of atomic forces.

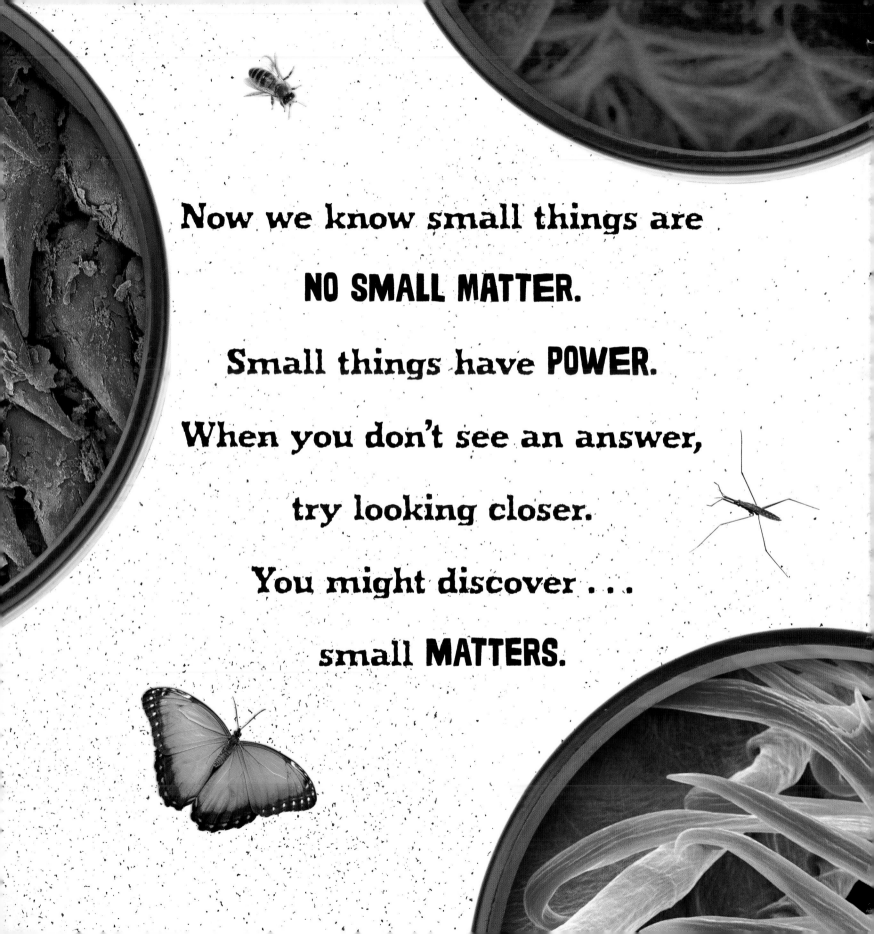

Now we know small things are

NO SMALL MATTER.

Small things have **POWER.**

When you don't see an answer,

try looking closer.

You might discover . . .

small **MATTERS.**

THE SCANNING ELECTRON MICROSCOPE

Since its invention in the 1590s, the microscope has helped us see small things more clearly. The first of these scientific tools was the light microscope (also called an optical microscope). But a light microscope can only zoom in so far.

The scanning electron microscope (SEM) was invented in 1937. It offers an even closer look at small things. It does this by mapping an object's shape with a beam of tiny particles called electrons. SEMs took the zoomed-in photos you see in this book.

Inside a SEM, a heated wire causes electrons to jump off their atoms (the basic stuff that everything is made of). Freed electrons are carefully guided down a column using a series of magnetic lenses. This process focuses the electrons into a narrow beam. The beam enters a part of the microscope called the sample chamber where it scans an object the researcher wants to see. As it scans, electrons bounce off and the microscope's detectors collect them. A computer uses this information to put together a SEM image. Color is often added to the image to highlight details. A SEM image may magnify an object 10,000 times, 100,000 times, or even more than that.

THE NANOSCALE

How small are the things we see through a SEM? Small enough to be measured on the nanoscale! The nanoscale refers to things measured in nanometers. A nanometer is one billion times smaller than a meter. Imagine this: if a meter were as wide as Earth, then a nanometer would be as wide as a marble.

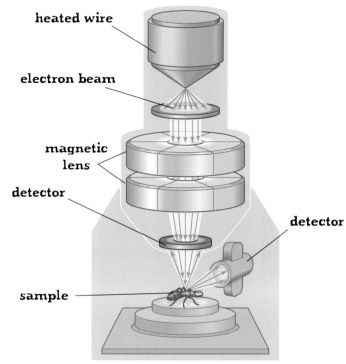

heated wire

electron beam

magnetic lens

detector

detector

sample

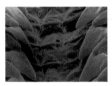

SNAIL TEETH

A snail's tongue has thousands of teeth on it that shave at its meal like a mini cheese grater. The teeth of a limpet sea snail are the strongest material made by any animal. They are formed of extremely thin mineral fibers, including iron. These teeth are nearly indestructible.

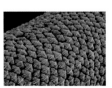

SHARK SKIN

A shark might appear to be silky smooth, but its skin is actually sandpaper rough. Zoom in and you'll see thousands of small, toothy scales. A closer look shows that these scales have ridges. The ridges allow water to flow smoothly over the shark's skin. This helps a shark swim fast.

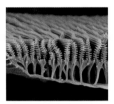

BUTTERFLY WINGS

An open blue morpho butterfly wing looks bright blue, but it's actually brown. The wing is covered in rows of scales made up of tree-shaped structures that bend light into different colors. The structures keep most of those colors trapped, but blue reflects out as a radiant shimmer.

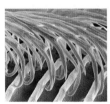

BIRD FEATHERS

A bird's feathers are strong, light, and perfectly shaped for flying. Flight feathers have a spine down the middle and two sides of delicate strands called barbs. These barbs join together with nano-sized hooks. When a bird isn't flying, it spends lots of time zipping its loose barbs back together.

SNAKE SKIN

A snake's skin helps it slither along in just one direction—forward. Snake skin has overlapping scales that face toward the tail as well as tiny rough ridges along the belly. These structures push against the ground and grip, creating friction. This stops the snake from slipping.

WATER STRIDER LEGS

The water strider does what might seem impossible: walking on water. It spreads its weight out over six long legs covered with hairs. These nano-sized hairs press down lightly on the surface of the water. Since they don't apply much force, the water just bends around each tiny hair, leaving the strider standing in dimples.

BEE HAIRS

A bee's eye is covered in hairs that are spaced perfectly to keep out sticky pollen grains. The hairs hold the pollen out at their tips, far from where it could hurt a bee's eye. A bee cleans its eyes (and whole body) often. It carries the brushed-off pollen back to the hive to be used as food.

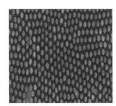

CAT TONGUES

A cat's tongue is covered in back-curving spines made of the same stuff as fingernails. These spines act as a built-in comb when a cat licks its fur, keeping the animal neat and clean. Cats of all sizes like to stay clean so their prey won't smell them sneaking closer.

CICADA WINGS

Cicadas have wide, waxy wings dotted with cone-shaped bumps that are super at shedding water. Water beads up on top of the bumps and—bonus!—the water picks up dirt, dust, and pollen. Before long the water drops join with others, get bigger, and pop off. This leaves the wing both dry *and* washed.

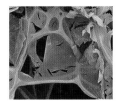

TOUCAN BEAKS

What tropical bird is one-third beak? The toco toucan! It flies around with a head full of luggage but never drops into a nosedive. The toucan's huge beak is lighter than it looks. The beak is made of a loose, lacy framework. Each bony frame is sealed with a film like the skin of a drum, which makes the beak light and strong.

GECKO TOES

Even though its feet aren't sticky, a gecko can cling to almost anything. The secret is in its toes! Each toe has many thousands of tiny hairlike structures. At the end of each of these structures are hundreds of nano-sized bristles that are like even finer hairs. Van der Waals forces cause a slight attraction between molecules of the bristles and molecules of the surface they're touching. Put a billion nano-sized forces together and—presto!—you get a stick-to-it gecko.

FURTHER READING

Ben-Barak, Idan. *Do Not Lick This Book*: *It's Full of Germs*. New York: Roaring Brook, 2017.

Davies, Nicola. *Tiny Creatures: The World of Microbes*. Somerville, MA: Candlewick, 2014.

Hall, Kirsten. *The Honeybee*. New York: Atheneum, 2018.

Heos, Bridget. *Shell, Beak, Tusk: Shared Traits and the Wonders of Adaptation*. Boston: Houghton Mifflin Harcourt, 2017.

Huber, Raymond. *Gecko*. Somerville, MA: Candlewick, 2019.

Stewart, Melissa. *Feathers: Not Just for Flying*. Watertown, MA: Charlesbridge, 2014.

Waxman, Laura Hamilton. *Toco Toucans: Big-Billed Tropical Birds*. Minneapolis: Lerner Publications, 2016.

PHOTO ACKNOWLEDGMENTS